TheYamaSystem.com

ISBN: 979-8-9852024-0-3

Designed and edited by Matt Clark
alimat-inc.com

THE JOURNAL JOURNEY

JOURNEY

MATT LUCAS

WHAT'S INSIDE

⚛ INTRODUCTION

Have you ever thought, "How do I think?"

The rule is "what is constant isn't conscious." Journaling is a tool I've used for 30 plus years to remember that I'm a thinking being. I won't bore you with quotes, but I'll throw out a favorite that I use as mantra – not to motivate, but to teach.

"If you can't walk with it, it doesn't exist."
- Shaolin Wisdom

I believe in liberation through limitation. Many of the exercises in this book are designed to limit you in order to challenge and stimulate your creativity and expand the lenses into the ways you think. When you learn anything new it's good to have simple tools and exercises to start you off. With journaling and writing, these simple tools are a good way to keep up this work regularly, and keep it interesting. There's a reason psychics and astrologers stay in business. They talk about *you*.

Journaling is a great way to organize your thoughts and refine your world view. It's also a way to purge and organize your thoughts so you can have actual conversations with people instead of making them sit there like hostages while you vent or process your life at them. It will help especially when you need to communicate something important, so that when you *do* reach out, you may actually get your point across. Remember that these are ideas, not laws. One of the first things you should tune into is how much you adhere to structure.

For example, there are some great breathing techniques that can help you calm down under stress. However, if you are the kind of person with a mindset fixated on "doing" and "doing it right," techniques can actually cause you more stress because you're too focused on following the rules. This is your path. Do the work and discover all the ways you can approach the same idea.

As I put together this course I looked at shelves full of old journals. I started writing around 11 years old. At first it was simple reporting and complaining. Then I got righteous, writing about how everyone else was wrong and I was right! Oh... and lots of stuff about girls. Then I became a songwriter. For a good 20 years my writing was just short stories that ended up becoming more cryptic and everything rhymed. Now I'm more instructional and free form. Just writing to write. Sometimes fiction, sometimes recapping the day, sometimes two hours, sometimes five minutes.

Throughout this book we'll go over ways to integrate this work into your day, with the practice course as well as some exercises to keep this work "Phresh." If you are into one particular exercise and it really inspires you, stay with it. Keep the others in your back pocket for when you are stumped, or could use a catalyst.

Let's get started.

Go to **TheJournalJourneyCourse.com**
and get all of this in video form.

REPORTING

When you first start journaling, the simplest way is Reporting. This is the how, why, when, what, and where of your life. You can get even deeper into it with what I call the 5/3/5 formula: 5 questions, 3 lenses, and 5 senses.

THE

5/3/5

FORMULA

5 QUESTIONS

HOW   WHY   WHEN   WHAT   WHERE

3 LENSES

EXTERNAL   TRIVIAL   INTERNAL

5 SENSES

SIGHT   SOUND   SMELL   TOUCH   TASTE

EXTRA CREDIT: INTUITION

Literally start at the beginning of the day and recap till the end. There are layers to this. First, there's the timeline.

I am a huuuuge music lover and I feel that the lyric "woke up this morning" has been used enough. Personally I feel like anyone who has written it into a song after the year 1952 is an uncreative hack. However, we are journaling, and yes it's your life. All I ask is that if you write "woke up this morning... got bills to pay," please just don't sing it.

Five Questions: How, why, when, what, and where.
This is one of the simplest ways to report. You can be broad and just talk about your day:

How was your day? **Why?**
When did you get up? **When** did you get to work? **Why?** How?
When did you eat? **Where?**
What happened today?

You get it.

You can even be *more* specific. Let's take making coffee as an example.

How did you make it? French press? Did you buy it? Why?
When? Before you left? Or on the way to work?
Where? A coffee shop, in your kitchen?
What kind of coffee? Was it tea? Then why are you writing about coffee?

Three Lenses:
Remember this is about you reporting your life, and we are all creatures of habit. Even if you have an exciting life of travel and constant adventure, you still probably have your daily habits. The way you pack your suitcase, or the way you set up camp. Then you have your preferred point of view. Some people love the sights, some love the sounds, others love the vibe. So explore your report through the following three lenses:

External:
What you see, what you do, the people you meet, and the places you go. Imagine if you were a camera: What does it see?

Internal:

How do you feel? How is it to wake up today vs. yesterday? Are you excited? Traffic! Again? This is an even deeper dive into you as a person. Remember that a feeling or emotion is literally just an opinion-based reaction. For example, I've been doing martial arts for 40 years. I have seen it transform individuals into empowered and peaceful people, all by punching and choking each other. If you were abused, you may associate martial arts with violence, and fighting. Fun fact: We're both right. Some of my best students were abused, beaten and assaulted, but through a martial arts practice their past associations have completely transformed. How did you feel about traffic today? Did it stress you out or did listening to an amazing audio book make the drive seem effortless? When you write it all down you'll get to experience how your opinions and lenses change.

Trivial:

It's the trivial little things that make up your life. Sure we all wake up, we all have bills to pay, we all brush our teeth. But, do you use an old-school tooth brush because that's what your dad who's a dentist used to give out for free, or do you use a $200 electric one? Do you start your day with coffee or tea? I personally roast my own coffee, so I'm constantly trying new beans and flavors. What are the trivial things in your life?

Reporting from the senses.

When you report from the senses it's easy to get stuck on just one, but there are so many more to tune into! It's not really the truth until all the senses are involved. When you are describing your morning, how does it change when you wake up to the smell of breakfast cooking vs. to the sound of a loud crash in the other room? When I'm reporting I often make it a point to take a moment and go through all my senses as well as tuning into my other lenses. Does it smell different at work when the janitorial crew is there? How do your sheets feel? During fire season in California you can taste the air. You get the point.

EXERCISE ONE

Report on a moment of your day.
Start broad and external, then get trivial, then internal.
Use the 5/3/5 formula.

For example:

External
The alarm went off at 6 a.m.

Trivial
I left the window open last night and it was freezing in my room this morning.

Internal
It's hard to get out of bed when it's cold.

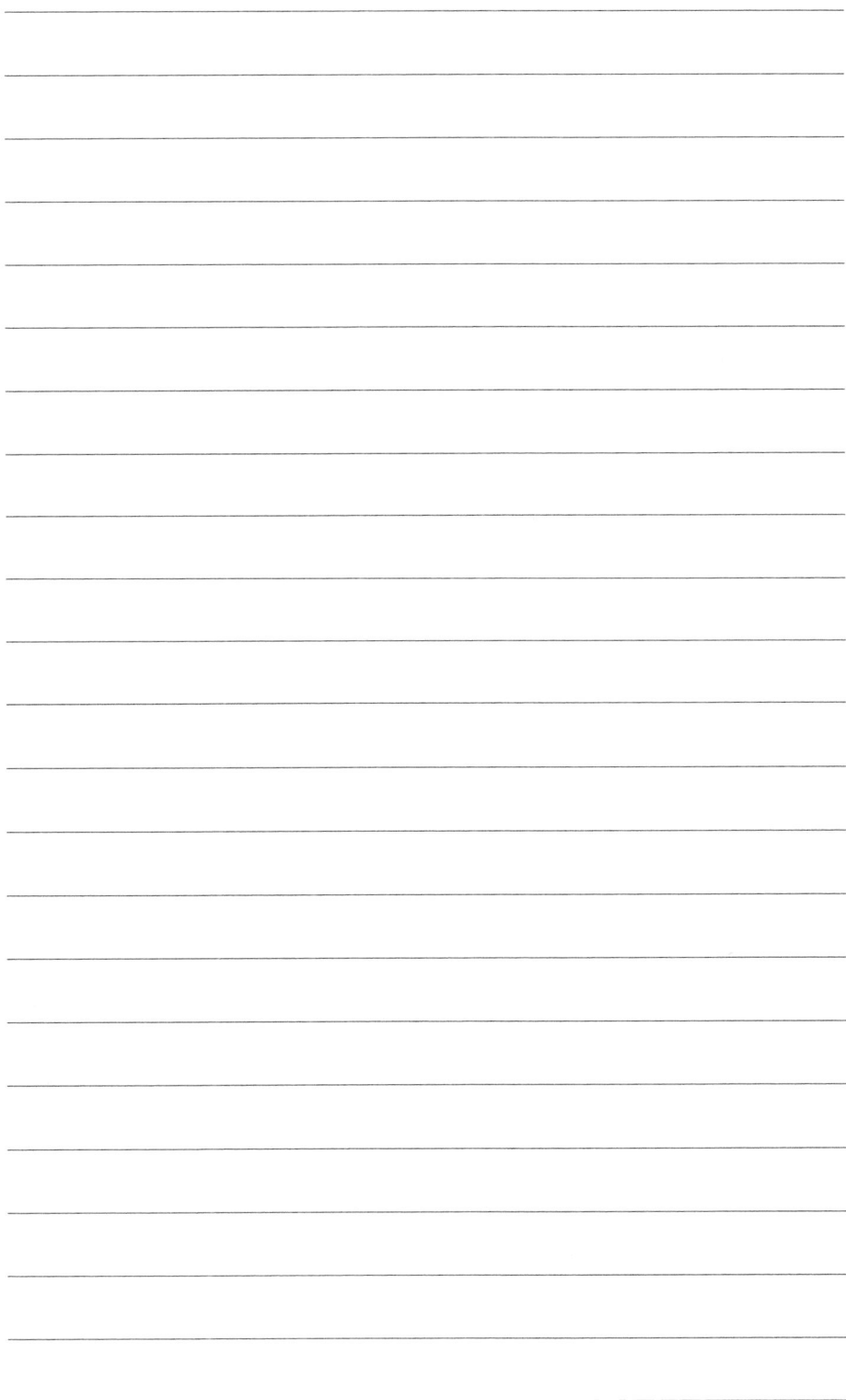

EXERCISE TWO

How many other ways can you say "woke up this morning?"
Or is it even necessary? (No singing please.)

Examples:

- My day started at 6 today.
- I beat my alarm today.
- 6 a.m. snuck up on me.
- It was nice to sleep 'til the sun was out.

Practice reporting the same thing but from different aspects of the
5/3/5. Sure you woke up, but how did the air feel, the bed, your body?
Did you wake up stressed? What was the first thing you saw? If you are
reporting at the end of your day, how many routines do you repeat daily?
Now report them in different ways. 5/3/5!

EXERCISE THREE

Flip the Script
Now instead of reporting what you did, report what you are about to *do*. Flip the script.

Why?
The formula for integrity is basically aligning your thoughts, words and actions. In some cases, reporting at the end of the day may create guilt (weight loss comes to mind). However, if you keep a journal in the kitchen and write down what you are about to eat and report how you feel about it, you will realize that you have the knowledge to move towards your goal. I admit this isn't a report as much as a to-do list. However, you can make it a report by doing it. Thoughts, words, and actions!

Simply write a goal on ten pieces of paper and report what you're about to do. Then look at the goal you just wrote and ask, "is this moving me towards that goal?"

It's generally best to answer just yes or no. If you start bargaining or justifying, it's usually the first sign that you are about to fall out of integrity.

RANT

I HATE THE DESERT

AND

RAVE

BUT I LOVE SEDONA

Rant and Rave plays a few roles in my life and work. I've used it for journaling as well as building rapport and empathy with everyone from yoga practitioners to homicide detectives.

This chapter is to begin the process of witnessing and refining who you are and your own views by expressing your opinions. You'd be surprised by how much easier it is to connect with others and their point of view when you take a little time to connect with your own. How is your rapport with yourself?

Feel free to express yourself using the 5/3/5 formula, and then let go of any idea that you or your opinions are set in stone. If we are living consciously, we are always transforming and evolving. Look at how opinions changed about Elvis. He was too provocative for TV at first, yet he was considered positively wholesome compared to artists like Ice Cube in the 90's. These days Ice Cube is starring in family movies and the cycle repeats itself. Express, purge, witness, and purify your thoughts and feelings through this work. You may find that some aspects of your point of view are as dated as an 80's haircut, while others are consistent throughout your whole life. Some may even be ahead of their time. Either way, they're yours, make peace with that.

These days everyone *loves* to complain and focus on the negative. Fortunately, a good rant is always a great catalyst to start the writing process. No bar or nightclub ever cleared out because two people were getting along in the parking lot.

LEVEL ONE

 **3 MINUTES**

RANT

Set a timer for three minutes and find a point in your day that you can rant about.

Maybe something happened that annoyed you, or maybe you just want to let off some steam. Tune into your senses. Did you hear something? Couldn't get a moment of silence, or even hear yourself think? How was dinner? How was the service? The parking? How did your food taste? How did it feel?

Remember, focusing on the senses tunes you into the truth of your experience. This is your story and it can be exotic or mundane. Just make it personal.

That said, I can rant about brunch or K-pop for an infinite amount of time. Gross.

LEVEL ONE

 **3 MINUTES**

RAVE

Reset your timer and rave about something you love!

What are you stoked about? What inspires you? Did you hear some good music or kind words? Did you taste some good food? Go for a swim? Smell the sea?

Think of all the things that happened today. Then choose one and rave about it.

LEVEL TWO

Once you've written your first set of Rant and Rave, the next level is to flip the script. Rave about what you were ranting about and rant about what you were raving about. This is good perspective and empathy training.

My most recent personal example of flipping the script is related to Iron Maiden and Guns-N-Roses having both released new studio recordings this month. I can rave about both of those bands and how it's great that they're still making new music. I can also rant about how the music is boring crap and lacks any soul.

When I've worked this in rooms with people like cops or at-risk- youth, they've often been afraid to talk. It may have been shyness, or an actually unsafe environment, so I usually began by giving a quick on the spot cue. I'd say, "On three, what's one thing you could rant and complain about endlessly?" Then do the same with a rave.

The point is not to overthink it.

⏱ 3 MINUTES

Write each rant and rave on a separate page.

Do two rounds of Rant and Rave and two rounds of flipping your script.

- 3 minutes of rant
- 3 minutes of rave
- 3 minutes of flip your rant
- 3 minutes of flip your rave

RANT

RANT

RANT

RANT

RAVE

RAVE

RAVE

RAVE

FLIP YOUR RANT

FLIP YOUR RANT

FLIP YOUR RANT

FLIP YOUR RANT

FLIP YOUR RAVE

FLIP YOUR RAVE

FLIP YOUR RAVE

FLIP YOUR RAVE

LEVEL THREE

10 MINUTES

Commit to ten minutes and set a one-minute timer.
Alternate from rant to rave each minute.

RANT, RAVE, REPORT

Now that we understand concepts and lenses, bringing them together is the beginning of point-of-view and empathy training. It's the tool that has brought me out of many states of paralysis throughout my life.

For example, as I am putting together this course I am on an "adventure." Needing to get some time alone, I have built out a vehicle to take me out into the wilderness where I am writing and editing and will emerge smelling like "time," and looking like an Appalachian home-schooled kid from the eighties. By the time you are reading this, I will have a complete course on journaling. Why? Because I am out here writing every day, morning, noon, and night! I am practicing physical training as well, so there is a lot to rant, rave, and report about.

Here's an example.
Allow me to rant, rave, and report about the lamest two days I've had in a long time. I was left feeling defeated and lost, along with heart-pounding stress taking over my psyche.

Rant:
I hate the desert. No seriously, I hate it. It makes me feel trapped, it's lifeless, it's hot, it's inhospitable and all that's there are drug addicts, white people wanting to be "free" and folks that just wanna F&%K S#!T UP!!!

Rave:
You can see the stars. The landscape can be vast and unique, sometimes alien-like. Also, there are no bears.

Report:
The desert is 106 degrees. It will take me about two days to get across it.

Rant:
I found dispersed camping. It was all rocks and of course, in the middle of the night, I heard shouting off in the distance. It was some meth heads living out in the middle of nowhere. During their fight their Pit Bull and German Shepard got loose and as I was working out I heard them running at me barking and growling. They tried to attack me, so I threw some stuff at them, jumped into my Jeep and slammed the door shut. They stayed outside for a couple minutes just barking and growling. Their body language told me they were in attack mode. At first I tried to find some treats for them, but it didn't work, so screw it, I pepper sprayed them. Since the dogs were between me and my tent, I also got some on the tent and I burned my eyes packing up to get the hell outta there.

Rave:
Hey, I got a story out of it! Not to mention, this still proves my argument that the desert is no good. I was cool under pressure and at least I had something non-lethal to chase the dogs away. A good right of passage often requires us to be uncomfortable and to act beyond our capacity. I feel this is a good start.

Report:
I was in the desert and some dogs got out. They ended up trying to attack me. I was able to fend them off, and get out safely. Then I found a lake, took a quick swim, and meditated.

Being able to rant, rave, and report about this scenario allowed me to get some things off my chest, then see it as a gift through raving about it. Since it's my journal I don't have to justify or try to add bravado. The report lets me see it from a place of training. S#!% happens and now I can be even better prepared for the next time something random and insane happens to me.

EXERCISE

 5 MINUTES

This exercise is about choosing the same thing to rant, rave, and report about. Choose a subject you can either rant or rave on and write for five minutes.

For example:

Subject I hate: The Desert
Rant: Hot as hell
Rave: Anywhere other than desert (yeah yeah, Joshua Tree, blah blah, don't defend it)
Report: A day in the desert

Subject I love: The Guitar
Rant: It never helped me meet girls
Rave: I've never been bored
Report: Six strings and some wood on my lap

We live in a very binary, often reactionary world. This is proof that we aren't experienced enough in our own point-of-view training to realize that when we truly experience something fully there is Yin and Yang present at all times.

When we see things for what they are and become aware of the many ways they can be interpreted, we often get to enjoy others' opinions even when we might disagree with them.

I hate the desert, but I enjoy hearing why you love it, and just because I judge your love for the desert, I don't really judge you as a whole. If someone has "bad" taste in music, it doesn't mean they're a bad person.

Or does it?

INTENTION

AND

OBSTACLE

Learning how to create habits is often the best way to begin to understand them. For instance, learning martial arts is a way to develop a skillset for peace through learning how to fight. We learn to fight so we don't have to. That said, if we learn the basic rules of drama, then perhaps we can learn to see when it's coming or how we create it.

Reporting is taking a play-by-play report, list, account, or description of something you've done, heard, experienced, or researched.

Relating it in story form is a way of finding the intention and obstacle of that report.

If you train with me, or we hang out together for at least 55 seconds, I will bring up "story." Very often we live and learn through story. However, story can also be the essence of our suffering. Cultivating a keen eye and relationship with "your story" is a skill that can open up your world view. Remember you have your story, and everyone else has theirs. Then there's the truth. The essence of suffering is when your story or "view" doesn't align with what's actually happening.

In "new age" terms. When "*your* truth" is misalignd with "*the* truth" it can create suffering. Even if it seems like it may be positive. There is no hard-and-fixed rule to this. Take American Idol auditions for example. See how many people are convinced they are great, but forget that performance requires real connection and more than just being able to entertain your family. They finally get in there, and it's ... awkward. Sometimes it blows minds and sometimes it just becomes an embarrassing meme. We've all heard the reports of how lottery winners often go broke. Why?

It's a misalignment.

Intention and Obstacle is the simple essence of turning a report into a story. Now don't confuse a story with rant or rave; those are just your opinions.

A story is different.

For example:

"Waking up and having a cup of coffee" is a simple report.
The intention is simple ... coffee.

Now let's see if there's an obstacle. When I say this, I am not asking you to focus on creating drama in your life. Remember to be mindful that some things are just simple and smooth, so there may not be any drama. However, this morning when I went to make coffee, I discovered I was out of beans, and wasn't sure if there was enough time to go out and get coffee before my Zoom meeting.

Now we have a story.

Here's another:

Intention: Coffee (and it all went smooth, it was all perfect)

Obstacle: Coffee this perfect always reminds me of "the one that got away." We met at a coffee shop in Spain when I was sitting alone again, having coffee. Now life has taken over and even my perfect coffee is merely a transaction.

Tuning into your intentions and obstacles are great ways to understand your world view and the ways you think as well as the ways you create stories around the things you experience. Even in your most logical, report-based thinking, you'll tend to tap into your creative mind to create some sort of meaning. In a life of seeking the truth, you'll often detour into a life of trying to create meaning.

How did you or how will you overcome the obstacle? Did the obstacle make you stronger, hinder you, or awaken you? Did the story resolve? How have you changed? This is your life, so the story doesn't have to have an ending. It can just be a story.

Remember that this can be as boring and mundane as you like. Mundane always takes the pressure off for me when I practice, so I suggest you start simply.

"I made coffee this morning. I was in a hurry so I turned on the water as I hopped in the shower. The handle was tipped over on the kettle so it melted. My new commercial range is hotter than I expected. I should get a new tea kettle."

Intention: Make coffee

Obstacle: Melted tea kettle handle

Transformation: Now aware of the power of commercial appliances

Resolution: Upgrade kettle, heck ... check on some of the other pots and pans too. Might as well go all in!

A simple story, with a simple resolution. There was no dragon, no big drama. Hopefully most of our lives are drama free. So ... what do we do when we have finally achieved perfectly balanced and drama-free lives but still want to dive deeper into cultivating our world view? Reversing this process is a good place to start.

How many times have you tried to dramatically explain something, or have something explained to you?

Imagine going to a doctor and when she asks you how you hurt your ankle, you tell her a long story about that time you were on an epic hike and on the way down you saw a snake cross the trail. You had to avoid it, but your friend freaked out. They ran into you and you twisted your ankle, crazy right? All the doctor is thinking is, "You coulda just said, I hurt my ankle."

I use the Intention and Obstacle exercise to discover the little things that I may not be mindful of while I'm in the middle of living my life. However I have found the biggest obstacles in my life are my own mind and my habits of creating intentions and obstacles. Personally, I have wanted to write a book for over a decade, and I have written many books worth of stuff. But what, you may ask, is my biggest obstacle?

It's me.

Through journaling and seeing my life through the lens of storytelling, it hit me: this obstacle is between me and me.

Tell your story. Be the hero, the villain, the narrator *and* the fly on the wall.

When I used to go out on tour, I'd sit at a coffee shop and listen to small bits of other people's conversations and I'd try and finish their stories. I would put myself in the mix. How could I resolve it? What if it was me?

Write down your day as a story and ask yourself: If I was watching this movie, what advice would I give this character? Think about what this character's quirk or secret is that could be their obstacle?

EXERCISE

5 MINUTES

Break up your writing into a simple five minutes of reporting, then five minutes of intention and obstacle.

FINDING
GAME

Search for the game that you are playing. Is there a throughline or a theme to your thoughts?

"Game" is the term I like to use for tuning into the intentions in your everyday life situations. We talk a lot about intention, but we often need to be aware of the little constants and trivial things we do that may or may not be working for us. This is the game. Remember, "what is constant isn't conscious."

In my mindfulness course I talk about "getting off autopilot." In journaling it's a good thing to take a little time to rediscover what is a constant in your life. This may be your game.

Once you are aware of your game, you can choose whether or not you want to partake in that particular game. Things have a tendency to ooze into your habits and you just go about your life as usual.

I may use the term "game," but this is really a mindfulness exercise.

Using the 5/3/5 formula ask yourself what you focus on, always asking why and how. Think about experiences you've had, or your plans for the future.

Here's an example of how I made my game absurdly obvious. Keep in mind that this work doesn't always have to be a deep self-help kind of exercise. You are allowed to make fun of yourself. In fact, sometimes you probably should.

I remember noticing that I always had my bag on my shoulder and looked like I was about to leave. My intention was to hang out, but the obstacle was that no one really felt connected to me or felt that I was at ease. If we were hanging out I would never just sit back and relax, I would never just take my bag off my shoulder. I remember writing about a girl I met and thinking about what kind of bag I'd have on my shoulder at our wedding. At my funeral, I would want to be propped up leaning out of the coffin with a bag on my shoulder. When I see all the different hard suitcases at the airport carousel I always giggle thinking "how the hell do these people fit those on their shoulders?"

The weirder and more absurd you get means that you are finally getting into the things that make you unique. Your story is yours, and it's the quirks and odd little details that make you different. Finding your voice and uniqueness is an entire life's path. Tell your story from as many sides as you can.

As an exercise, flip the script, or write from another perspective. Play another game. If my throughline is "wake up–make coffee" and I keep writing about how my body feels when I wake up and how I'm always rushed, that's my game. Use the 5/3/5 formula to break down the cause and effect, get to the essence of that habit or change it altogether. Am I playing this game in more parts of my life other than when I wake up? Maybe I should practice slowing down. We will get into this more in the next chapter.

"Wake up–make coffee" can be written about in so many ways. This is often the misconception about straight reporting. It may seem dull or straightforward but there is space within it for a ton of creativity. Reporting isn't just for non-fiction however. "I woke up confused … was I an awkward wizard kid, or a sexy vampire?" is not what I'm talking about.

Look at your game from the 5/3/5 perspective and find another way to either change it or get better at it.

What if your game is to wake up early and work out? At first you may be writing about the workout itself or keeping an exercise journal. Over time you can begin to write about how it feels throughout the day, the way your clothes fit, or how the space you train in looks. Report on your struggles. Write about a trivial new pair of sweatpants you're excited to sport. Write about how much more laundry you have to do now that you're always sweating. Have you met some new people? There are so many other aspects to a report, and so many ways you can see deeper into the games you're playing.

Finding your game is also a way to start taking responsibility for yourself, your habits, and your life. I remember a friend who went to the gym hoping to meet people but was always wearig headphones. When I asked why he didn't take them off, he said, "well everyone else wears theirs, so ..." His game was to do all that physical work to make himself attractive and to meet someone. But he was forgetting that he needed to open up his own space for others to enter. Our games are usually just us playing ourselves. I told him the owners should rename the place "Headphones Gym: Get fit alone on your 'phones."

EXERCISE: FIND YOUR GAME

Report your day, or read back through some old entries from past exercises. See if there's a throughline. Think about the 5/3/5 formula. Are you always asking why or how? Do you focus on the trivial things, brands, status, and feelings? Or are you more into the senses, like a wine connoisseur using as many adjectives as possible? Look for your throughline. You'll usually have at least one.

Now change your perspective. If you're always asking why or how, you can simply ask a different question or just make a statement. Why and how comes up alot during break ups. Really you should be admitting that you already know why and how. If focusing on the trivial is your game, then tap into your feelings or ask why that is your focus. I love asking wine connoisseurs to use their love of esoteric adjectives to describe something mundane, or to view the wine from an internal place, versus just the external.

Play the game on purpose so you don't play yourself.

GOOP

GOAL   OBSERVE   OBSTACLE   PLAN

LOOP

Journaling is a way to look at yourself and the ways you exist in your own life as well as the stories you tell. Now that you are getting the lay of the land, you can start building a toolbox. Right now, for instance, do you need some bear spray or a tissue? This technique is designed to help you take your stories and integrate them into action. You can make them real or change your game. Having a plan is like having an emergency kit. We are all less reactionary when we have a plan.

We all have goals. We go to retreats, sit in big banquet rooms, and walk across hot coals to get empowered in order to achieve those goals. But after all that, we get home and there is the comfy couch we sit on and watch TV. We sit in traffic, we go back to work, or we look in the mirror and the old habits pop back up like those bright yellow buoys in *Jaws*. Look just under the surface and there's the monster.

That's your obstacle.

You don't need a bigger boat, you need to make friends with that shark. Remember the 5/3/5 formula from "Reporting" while doing this practice.

GOAL:

Write down a simple goal you'd like to achieve

_____

_____

_____

_____

_____

_____

OBSERVE:

Now observe yourself achieving that goal, and write about it using the three lenses.

EXTERNAL:
How would it look?

INTERNAL:
Whether it's a plan or a thing or simply to be loved, how would it feel to achieve that goal?

TRIVIAL:
What are the little details? For example; Falling in love is universal, but it looks different to everyone. What are the details that will make your goal yours?

Did you use the 5/3/5 formula? *Observe, Dammit!*

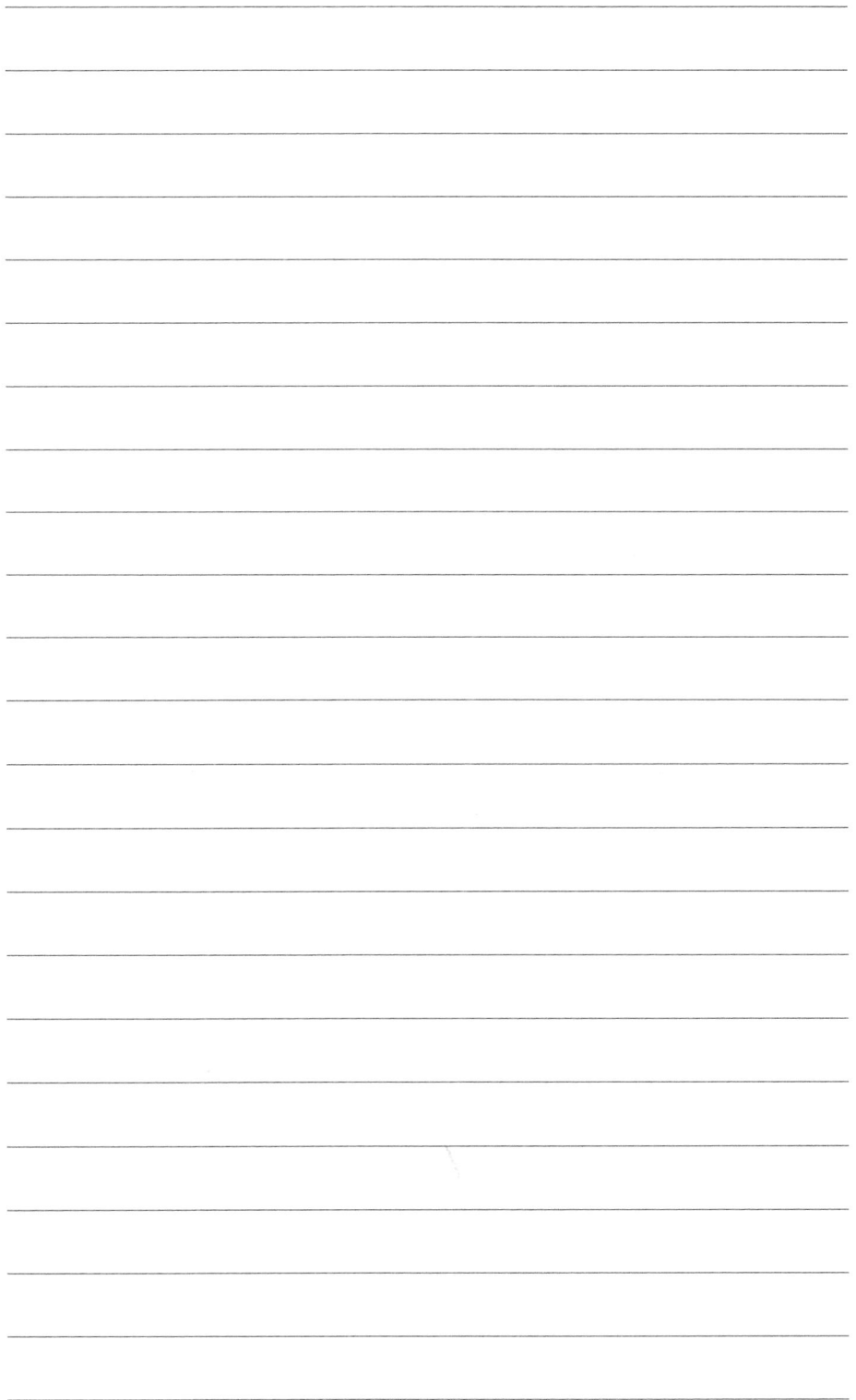

OBSTACLE:

Now get real for a sec. What's standing in your way?
Time? Energy? Money? Place? Your own mind? Fear? Overconfidence?

Write on it. Have fun with it.

I used to love poking fun at the internal demons that were always messing things up for me.

Make friends with your darkness and invite it into the light.

Look at it through the 5/3/5 formula.

_____

_____

_____

_____

_____

_____

_____

_____

_____

_____

_____

_____

_____

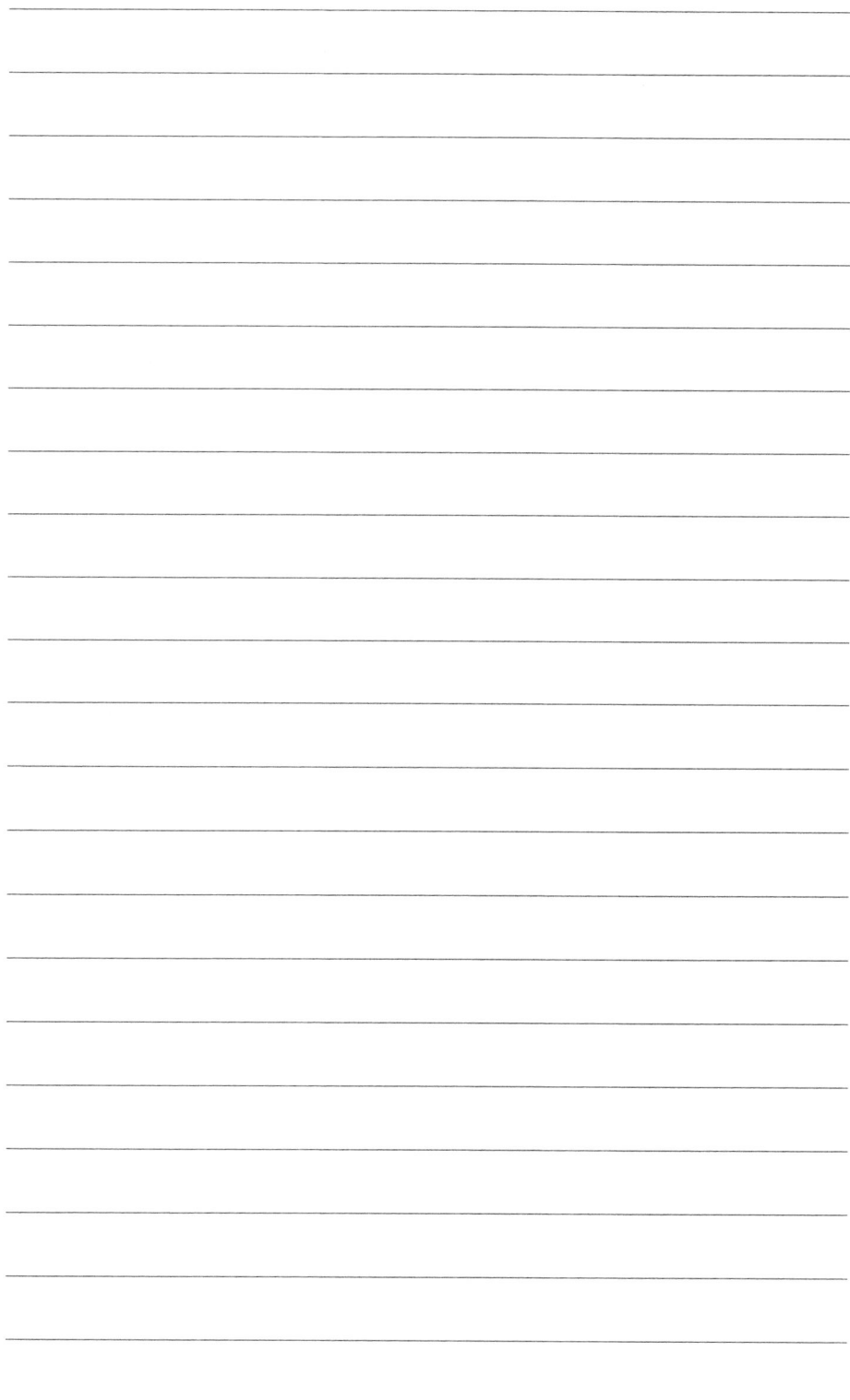

PLAN:

Now come up with an "If/Then" plan.

If _____ happens.

Then _____

This will help you spot your demons and have a plan when they show up to sabotage your goals.

I write on the same goal over and over – sometimes for months. Through reporting and using the different lenses and questions, I will read my report and ask if any of those obstacles have shown themselves. Now after years, I can finally spot them as they arrive. It took a while for me. Maybe you'll be faster.

Go through the GOOP Loop and keep repeating it in your journaling practice. Keep diving in deeper through the 5/3/5 formula.

Report your day through the lens of "am I moving towards my goal?" Then flip your script and change things up. Practice observing it from another perspective.

Have fun. Write a little every day.

_____

_____

_____

_____

_____

_____

_____

_____

THINKING **A** TO **C**

Thinking A to C is a process of stimulation-reaction-response. You can use this work as a way to get out of your reactionary brain and into your creative and responsive brain, the one that makes decisions and is a bit more you.

Humans are pretty predictable in their reactions. A snake oil salesman or a mentalist can predict what you may say next when they feed you a certain word or idea. For example, when put on the spot and asked to name a color, most people will answer "blue" or "red." If asked to name a vegetable there's a high probability that the answer will be "carrot." This is how marketing and social media works.

They need you reacting, not responding. Your emotions and reactions are easily manipulated, and yes, we all know that until we receive a stimulus that puts us back into a place where we "knew better," none of us are above an emotional reaction. With practice you can use this practice as a way to heighten your consciousness.

A great tool to get started is the random word generator. It's become my favorite inspirational tool. Just Google it or get an app.

Got it? Great, let's play a word association game.
Here's mine as an example:

Random word: Mom (A)

What is the first word that pops into your head when you see the word "Mom?"

Mine is "Call" (B)

Now write the next word that pops into your mind.

Mine is "Blanket" (C)

My sequence is this
A: Mom
B: Call
C: Blanket

This seems like a small thing but it's huge for creativity.

Now I'll will write on the word "Blanket" for five to ten minutes. I may bring it back around to "Mom", or simply report how my blanket feels when I wake up or go to bed. I can even turn it into a story.

Trivially, I can write on fabric choices, colors, or what a blanket means to me on a deeper level. I can write about how our culture is fixated on soft fake fur blankets. They're basically polyester and although soft, they don't breathe. Comfort = fake ... you get the point.

We love the superficial spectacle of the softness. However, over time there's no airflow, and OMG, the novelty chasing of our culture has me questioning our ability to make decisions for long-term health.

I could write for days on the trivial side of the word "blanket." Don't get me started on my feelings or actually stories that the blankets in my life could tell. Prom, the beach, or my friend's senile grandmother. Then there's the blanket that's been on this trip with me through 5,000 miles of mud. What used to be an Italian cashmere expression of luxury at my house now smells like a campfire and I don't know how I'm gonna get all the leaves, burrs and cactus spines out of it. BLANKET!!!!

The point of this practice is this: "A" is a stimulus, "B" is your reaction, "C" can be more of a conscious decision. This "A" to "B" reaction is what charlatans, snake oil salesmen, mentalists, magicians, and marketers use to understand how you think and make decisions in order to manipulate you. Being able to jump to "C" can carry more weight in your consciousness and decisionmaking that you could ever imagine.

Using your conscicus and creative sides to journal can take you to the next step on your path to cultivating a more discerning lens and world view.

Use your random word generator to pick a set of words and practice thinking "A" to "C."

Once you practice this drill, then your mind can skip "B" altogether and just jump to "C" naturally. Your mind will become sharp and quick. It's also a great way to break through writer's block.

Enjoy.

LEVEL ONE

 3 MINUTES

Generate three random words
Write your A, B, C sequence and remember, it's about responding not reacting.

A.

B.

C.

A.

B.

C.

A.

B.

C.

Now pick a C. and write about it for three minutes.

LEVEL TWO

 **30 SECONDS**

Generate ten random words and see if you can skip to C ten times in 30 seconds. (Repeat this a few times and practice often.)

A. _____   C. _____

A. _____   C. _____

A. _____   C. _____

A. _____   C. _____

A. _____   C. _____

A. _____   C. _____

A. _____   C. _____

A. _____   C. _____

A. _____   C. _____

A. _____   C. _____

A.

C.

A.

C.

A.

C.

A.

C.

A.

C.

A.

C.

A.

C.

A.

C.

A.

C.

A.

C.

A. _____

A. _____

A. _____

A. _____

A. _____

A. _____

A. _____

A. _____

A. _____

A. _____

C. _____

C. _____

C. _____

C. _____

C. _____

C. _____

C. _____

C. _____

C. _____

C. _____

A.

A.

A.

A.

A.

A.

A.

A.

A.

A.

C.

C.

C.

C.

C.

C.

C.

C.

C.

C.

HOW WOULD IT FEEL?

Most of the things I still do to this day are things that, if you were to have asked me at any other point in my life, I'd have said, "it's not my thing." Although it seems contradictory, I'm born to do this work.

Journaling was the tool that taught me how important it is to seek outside of my comfort zone for balance. My main state of joy has always been writing and being in a quiet creative space. I'm the furthest thing from an athlete, yet I've trained with and been a part of performing with super athletes. I hate competition, but I've competed against high-level martial arts practitioners. I'm shy and don't really like crowded places, yet I have been the front man of multiple rock bands and a professional performer since age 13.

Seriously, if you have ever met me, you'll know what I mean. I am *devoted*, even to the things I dislike because they balance me out. This is why journaling has played such a huge role in my life. It's also why I pursued these other paths on such a deep level. If you were to read my writing from age 24-32, you'd see that I was wondering if my choices were trying to destroy me. The practice of journaling has always been a way for me to check in with myself and keep on track.

One of the tools I use is to write about how I imagine it would feel to *want* to do something I find challenging. It is a meditation I learned in my martial arts practice about overcoming fear.

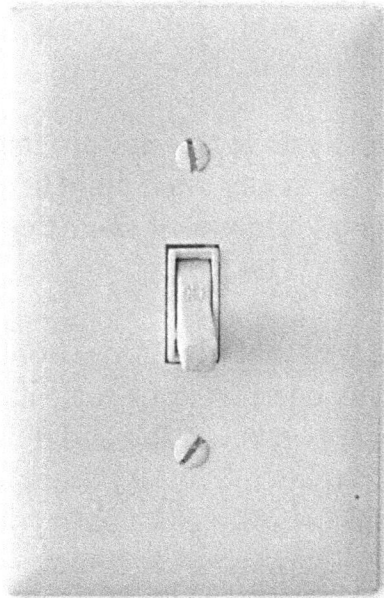

PRACTICE: TURN ON YOUR LIGHT

Find a comfortable place where you won't be disturbed. Lay on your back and just breathe.

Then, think about a scenario: a competition or something "grueling" that you are resistant to.

Now, imagine yourself bathed in and surrounded by a healing light.

Choose your color, (mine is usually light pink or a soft yellow).

Imagine that within that light you have the tools and the skills to accomplish your goal. In that light you are able to learn from your experience, to be heard, to be effective, and to adapt and thrive in that environment. Now really feel that feeling, and turn on your light.

In my martial arts practice it was easy for me to imagine the physical tools. However, through journaling, I realized that it was more than just martial techniques. It was about decision-making, emotional intelligence, focus, stretching, conditioning, and recovery. I understood that all those things could be carried into my day-to-day life.

I remember losing twice by getting the wind knocked out of me. I felt like I couldn't go on.

After that I used the light practice to experience how it would feel to have the tools to make it through such a lame feeling.

Once I really felt into it. I was able to move on to the next step.

The "If/Then Plan"

If I want to feel a certain way about an obstacle, and integrate this feeling into my life, *then* what do I need to do?

I used this practice and didn't get the wind knocked out of me again until I got older and met a giant dude that decided to hold me down and press his knee into my solar plexus while trying to crank my ear into my nipple. As a result of this training, that challenging interaction turned out to be just another weirdly enlightening experience.

DATING PROFILE

After a couple years of people complaining to me about how they could never find a partner, I started asking them how they were meeting people. Turns out, they were all trying to meet people online. Friends would often ask me to check out different peoples' profiles and ask me what I thought.

I started scrolling through the profiles and it hit me. All of them were too vague or too up for interpretation. They were meeting people who were already out of sync with their own expectations.

I noticed that basically everyone in the world of Internet dating "loves adventure."

We should all journal about what "adventure" means.

Most profiles of your typical "adventure" lover includes an infinity pool in an exotic locale.

Here's mine:
I had just come back from a week-long motorcycle camping trip through freezing rain, flying at 110 mph for 22 hours a day. The trip was only supposed to have been a one-day overnight to a spot about two hours away. But I was now over 1,200 miles away wondering if I could get my hands to work to unzip my zipper, or if I should just pee on myself and keep moving.

This is why it's important to define your preferences before you agree to that "adventure."

PRACTICE

Go on to a dating app, even if you're not looking to date. See what words people use that are extremely subjective and vague. Life has a broad spectrum. Take a moment and define where you are within those spectrums.

FUN: What's fun to you? To some, fun is going out drinking or partying at Mardi Gras. For others it's a potluck or a trip to Disney World.

Personally, I'd rather be at the DMV all day only to find that I don't have the right documentation than even think about Disney World or Mardi Gras. Hard pass.

Here are some other examples. Look around and come up with some of your own.

GOOD FOOD: Some love a great steak, and some are vegan. Are you a connoisseur of fine dining or do you consider yourself adventurous? Would you eat a bug?

ADVENTURE: Would you prefer to climb Everest or take an impromptu trip to wine country, (For me the wine country is a hell no. I'd rather eat bugs.)

TRAVEL: Live with an indigenous community in New Guinea for a year, or take road trip to Vegas? If you like travel, are you a novelty seeker or pleasure chaser? Maybe you are actually a homebody and a trip to the coffee shop is about your maximum travel commitment because you love your rad bed.

HARD WORK: Are you self-employed or do you have a steady job? If you work all the time, can you turn it off? I'm from a family of coal miners with an ex-Navy Seal for a dad, so if you ask what my definition of "hard work" is, in comparison to my family, I've never worked a day in my life. But to others I might look like a workaholic. Define for yourself what "hard work" is.

HOME: What is home to you? Is it in the city or in the woods, in the mountains or on the beach? Is it in the middle of the desert or just anywhere your family is?

SIMPLICITY: To some, simple is an all-expenses-paid trip where they don't have to think about anything. To others it's staying at home and working in the garden. Simple can be delivery every night and never having anything other than snacks in the fridge, while for others it's making dinner, watching a show, reading and getting to bed early. To some, simple just means they have a routine.

HEALTH: A healthy lifestyle can mean going to a hip fancy club and buying fancy smoothies or it can mean taking hikes, eating veggies, and having meaningful conversations. Healthy can mean eating the same boring thing every day or it can mean getting creative and nourishing yourself with fresh ingredients.

It's your life, so take a moment and define your preferences. When you do, you'll find yourself speaking with more conviction and having better conversations that can lead to finding your true community.

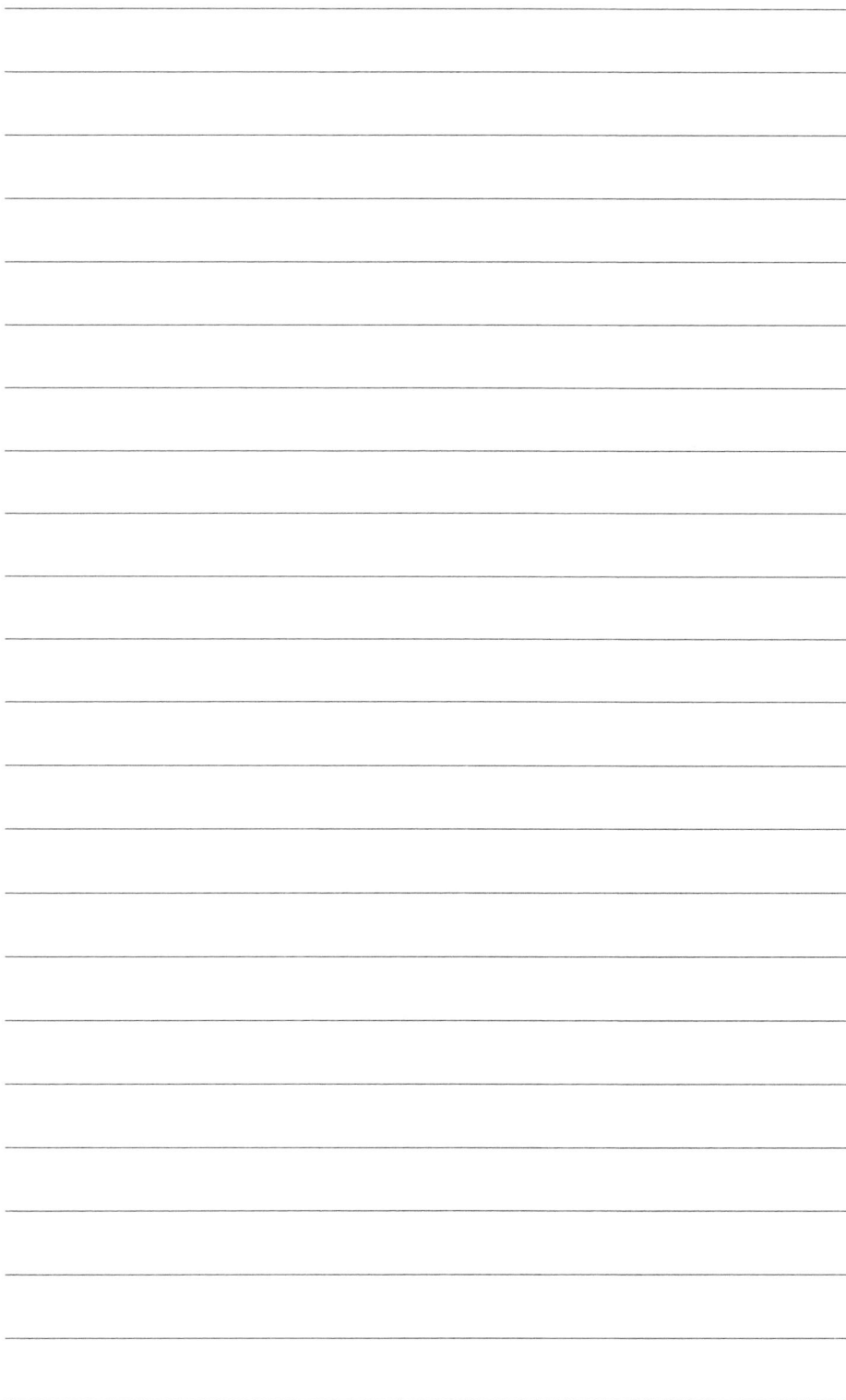

THIS ISN'T
SELF-HELP

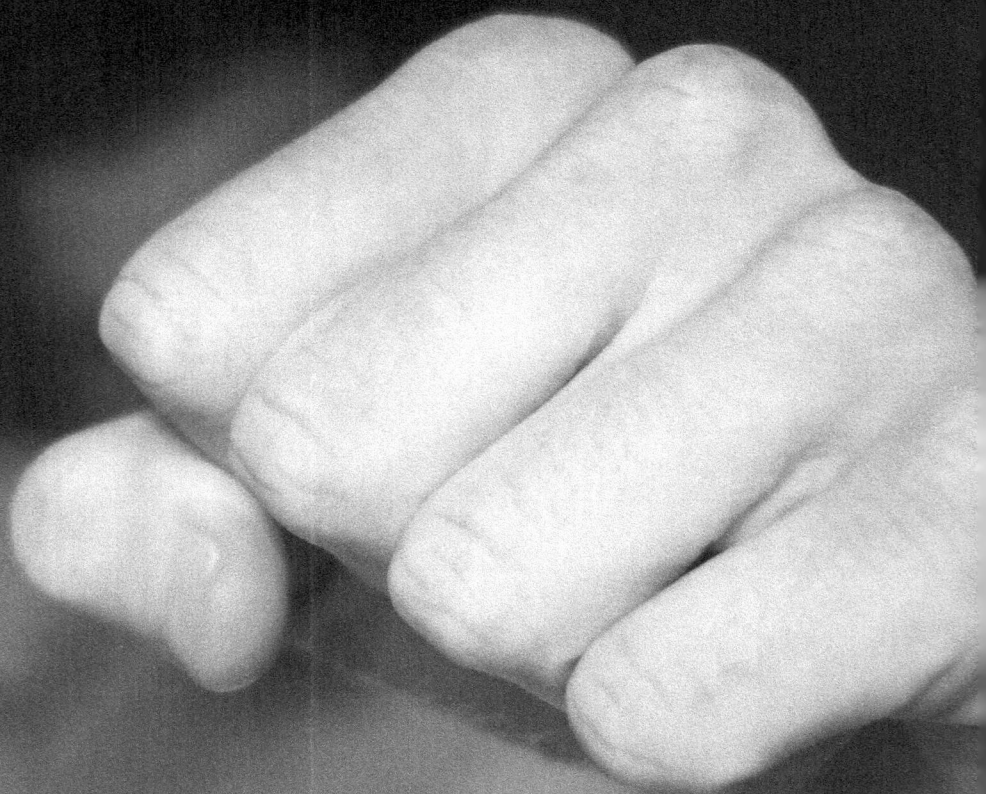

There's a virus infecting our minds and it's the obsession over self-help. Sometimes the best thing we can do for our inner peace is to just start moving towards actualizing who we really are.

Now that you've practiced reporting through your external, trivial, and internal lenses, it's important to remember that we often skip steps to discover who we are and how we view the world. It's easy to get trapped in envy, FOMO, or just trying out random lives. This is neither bad nor good, but it's often inefficient. Journaling isn't self-help. It's dialing in your preferences.

Write to discover and have your own revelations. It's easy to get caught up in "revelation porn," always looking for that "aha" moment. Those are easy. This is why so many self-help coaches lead with inspirational quotes. They are time-tested ways to motivate you – like a new band throwing in some cover tunes. You were tuning out the music and talking to your friends until they whipped out some *"Free Bird."* Are you truly inspired or are you in the presence of a spiritual wedding band?

Self-help comes from actualizing and truly discovering yourself. Observe and discover without judgment. This is why journaling is so valuable. I can remember writing on things that used to annoy me. Now I enjoy them. It's proof that we transform and change. If you are feeling trapped or stuck, know that things can and will change. Or if you feel that life is moving too fast you may realize that you can still be stuck and stagnant even if you are on a treadmill. Changing your perspective can snap you out of it. This is the magic of journaling.

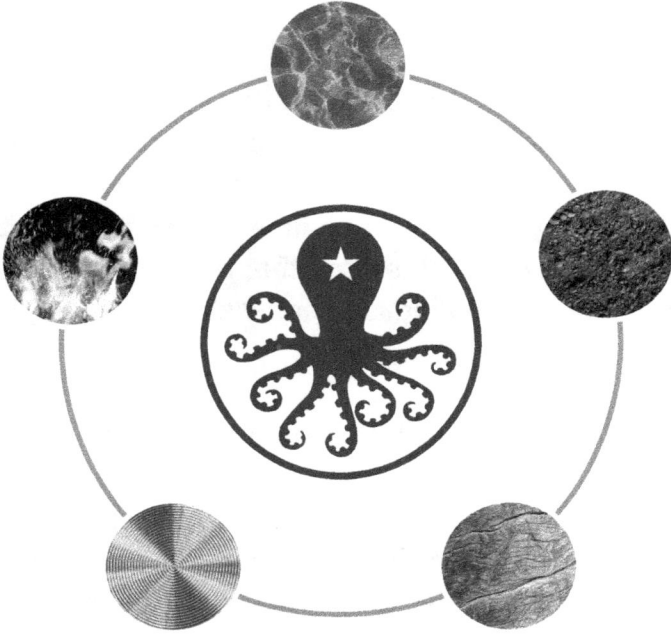

FIVE ELEMENTS

OF JOURNALING

EARTH

EARTH is stillness or slow moving. Think about the mountain, the tree, the glacier. With journaling, it's focusing on one idea. Take your time and feel. This takes me back to doing standing meditations for an hour in one position. You get time to feel into other parts of yourself or into nothing at all.

Write from a place of still focus. Sure, you woke up this morning, but how could you spend 20 minutes writing on that? Go deeper. Focus on the earthiness of it. The building of a mountain is slow. In your mind, slow down your movement to a glacier's pace. Then report, feel, and experience the senses. Take advantage of the mindfulness that Earth facilitates.

WATER

WATER is the flowing and adapting mind. When using this element to write, imagine journaling about your day and coming upon a problem or challenge. Water doesn't approach with might or ambition. It is the practice of changing and adapting your lens. Go around it, fill it in, flow under it and over it.

Water is the practice of flowing and becoming a part of something larger. See where you may want to adapt. Imagine that one drop of water is you. When added to a stream, you become that stream, which becomes a river, an ocean, then a cloud, then rain, etc ... It's about seeing through the lens of inclusion, flow, and adaptability.

When you write and the water element is present, think about how your tiniest movement can affect the larger whole. See things from many sides without resistance and ask questions, knowing that we are all in this together.

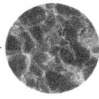

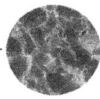

WOOD

Imagine the sprouting of a plant. It grows roots, then starts reaching towards the sun. It is flexible and bendable, always stretching and reaching up and down at the same time.

Journaling from the place of **WOOD** is the remedy to flying away into woowoo land. Have your sprout of a revelation, but sink your roots into the Earth too. This is the practice of being your own shaman, for lack of a better term. What roots you? Now stretch. This means to write from a place of inspiration inside your life now.

Knowing this can bring you into inspiration while keeping you from being overwhelmed. Your "big idea" is a tree. Now write from the perspective of a growing tree. No tree grows from planted seed to tree in an instant. It finds its roots, then sprouts and keeps growing and reaching. The larger the tree gets, the deeper the roots go. This is why so many ideas never amount to anything substantial. They are just, as author Liu Ming has said: "revelation porn" – a tree with no roots.

Refinement of an idea and education are **METAL.** This is writing from a place of research, whittling down into a refined place. Focus on an idea and refine it. Read on it then write more. Edit, make it slick.

Sometimes when I'm short on ideas, I will refine an old piece of writing. I will write instructions or lists, I will report something from a place of simplifying it and making it better and more refined. Metal is good for updating and refining an old journal piece that has become relevant and you feel like sharing it.

FIRE

FIRE is all about getting creative. Once we have done enough exercises and learned enough tricks, it's nice to be unbound by rules and see what comes up.

Be free, random, or even fictitious. I imagine fire in martial arts as the difference between running drills, then getting in a street fight. It can be sloppy and shapeless. However, if we have the other elements of Earth, water, wood, and metal on our side and have practiced enough, we can make fire solid and substantial. The tools and tricks are there to help us out of jams.

Basketball players in a game are fire. Sitting down at your computer and just writing free-form from a basic idea and seeing where it goes is fire. Creativity is fire, chaos is fire. Since this an esoteric metaphor, let it grow and engulf everything.

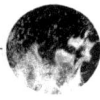

In art, we need creativity. The Five Elements are a way to illustrate different ways of looking at one thing. This practice is also a way to test whether we have integrated a skill or concept fully, both physically and mentally. Exercises get you working, but failing to *integrate* this work is what kills most people's practice. This is why the Five Elements are so important.

The most common example of failure to integrate is Art School. I regularly meet people who, when surrounded by artists, bring up the fact they *"used to"* study art, took an art course, or maybe even went to art school. However, now they aren't making art anymore. This is common for athletes too. I remind people that in these courses, just as in art school, or on a team, there is a teacher, a coach, or a leader who usually gives the challenges. Many people stop creating art after art school because in reality, they were *doing assignments* or *fulfilling requirements* in order to get the reward, the grade, the certificate or the degree they wanted.

Same goes for athletes. They are training to get the trophy, score the point, or get to the pros. The reward is obvious, external, and, to be honest, rather superficial. This is not a judgment; this has been my experience talking with thousands of people for over 30 years. The real judgment is the self judgment of feeling like a quitter, a fraud, or feeling discouraged because there is no one left to please other than ourselves. There is no reward other than the creation itself. This is why this work is *so damn rad!*

The next level to our creativity and self-discovery isn't the skill to create the art. Access to the next level comes from the creativity to create the *inspiration* for the art. There are no more assignments. The assignment is to *feel*, to develop your own lens, and to communicate *that*. This is when we graduate from **traditional art** into the **tradition of art.** Traditional arts are the classics. We study them. They are our fundamentals; great writers, classical or traditional folk songs, traditional martial arts. The tradition *of* art is the ability to communicate through your own lens with the tools that you have. This is why you are journaling – to discover your lens, your opinions, your preferences and your tools. You can be just as creative organizing your desk at work as a musician is writing a song. You just need to view it as *you*. When you know your preferences in this world you can make choices. You can think "A to C" and consciously move towards what you want. Think of how many people go on date after date and can't seem to find the right person. Maybe they should journal and figure out what they actually want, then report their day and discover if they are being the thing they want as well. If you want love ... are you loving? That starts with figuring out who you actually are.

The Five Elements are ways to dive even deeper into this. There really is no assignment with these – just keep the Five Elements in your mind, and use them to integrate ideas fully. These are concepts and frameworks. Ask yourself these questions when you are writing on an idea, or cultivating a skill, or just wanting to expand your lens.

Have you gone slow and stayed focused on the fundamentals?

EARTH

If you want something to write about, write from a grounded place. What are your fundamentals? What is the soil you are growing from? I have personally written about the same things for years. Imagine how many songs, poems, stories, and lives have revolved around the fundamentals of love, sex, and partnership. Without one of those you wouldn't be here. Honestly, most songs are just about sex or politics. What is the constant thing in your life that is the foundation you are standing on? What is the foundation of your job, your relationships and your family? How can you write, meditate, or communicate that? That is Earth.

Are you flowing through ideas and adapting to your space and environment, trying things out? Or are you stuck, stagnant, or fixated?

WATER

Where there's pain there's fixation; where there's fixation there's pain. This is the fundamental mantra of the healing arts. Be like water. If something is bothering you, think "A to C," or imagine it from another point of view. Adapt, or ask yourself what other ways are there to adapt. No judgments, water doesn't judge. Actually nature doesn't judge. Judgment is a human thing. Sure, water flows around, through, or engulfs something. But don't forget that it also takes the shape of the object it's in. Even the smallest drop of water can join with an ocean and blend. You are just as much a part of the entire world as a single molecule is a part of the ocean. This is water. Think big, adapt, then think small. It's all the same.

Have you taken the time to extend the smallest idea, sprouted a new one, been inspired? Or have your ideas become stunted because you're not growing yourself?

WOOD

You have your Earth and your water, but what is growing from these elements? How are you extending up and out? Remember the sprout of an idea can be a poem or "I feel like making soup." Then reach up with that idea. What kind of soup? Grow your roots deeper. Do you have a pot big enough for soup? Do you have access to the ingredients of that amazing soup you had on vacation? Start from there.

Have you taken time to refine or research or find a teacher? Or are you wafting around like a plastic bag on the highway?

METAL

You may be running out of energy or exhausted from your constant creativity. So make a list, make a plan, or read something and do some exercises on that. Go back to thinking "A to C," or "Rant and Rave." Write about a project that you may want to dive deeper into. Think about how you could refine it. Write your week's menu, plan your workouts, do math. I don't know ... it's your life, but refine. Metal is all about precision.

How often have you just let go and gotten creative in your life?

FIRE

Remember to consume everything in your path. Are you under pressure, and pressed for time? Are you sick of structure and in need of release? Are you pissed off or madly in love? This is fire! Can you let it consume you and then take control of it? In martial arts you learn, you refine, you run drills. Then you spar, or you may have to fight. In music you learn scales and songs. You practice endlessly. Then you get with your friends or you get up on a stage and you play.

With journaling you can train your inspiration, and cultivate your lenses. These skills become strong with practice and repetition, then you can sit down and write about anything and everything. Remember fire not only consumes, it purifies.

INTEGRATION

We all have our rhythm and nobody likes an evangelist. The more you get out and meet people, the more you dive into different perspectives you'll start seeing that some people wake up and workout, some wake up and read, some wake up and meditate. It's all about finding your timing.

Finding your own rhythm is the key to consistency.

For more on this check out my course on three methods
of practice at **TheYamaSystem.com**

The following are some ways you can start finding your rhythm.

TIME: Try writing at different times. Set a place in your home for writing. Make it easy, accessible, and simple: Use a pen and journal, type on a computer, or you can get all hipster with an ol' timey typewriter. Learn to feel when inspiration is there. You are your space. The main space that requires preparation is your own head, which is attached to your body, so how do you prep that?

MEDITATION: Take a minute of stillness or contemplation first ... just breathe. Then write free form for a few minutes.

MOVEMENT: Try writing after a workout. Clearing out and honoring your physical state will help you to focus on your inner experience.

FRESH START: Keep a journal next to your bed and make it the first thing you do. Write down your dreams, or make lists and outline plans.

FINAL THOUGHT: End your day with writing. Clear out your thoughts so you can start fresh tomorrow.

WALKABOUT: Put a journal in your pocket and just take a walk or a hike. When you see a nice spot or get an idea, stop and write it down.

NAP TIME: The good ol' method of sitting in a chair with an aluminum pan between your feet. Cup your hands and put a coin or marble in your palms. Place your hands on your lap and take a nap sitting up. When you begin to fall asleep your hands will relax and the coin will fall into the pan. Wake up and write the first thing that comes to your mind.

Thomas Edison was very fond of this technique. It allows you to access your hypnagogic state (Google it!) where problems often get magically solved. Extra credit for setting your mind on a particular problem or idea before you drift off with the intention of having an answer when the coin drops and you wake up.

DICTATION: Use voice dictation software and call someone you have deep conversations with and record it. You can also get the audio of your conversations transcribed. There are some great, affordable, and easy to use services online these days. I've found it especially helpful during meetings about creative projects or brainstorming sessions. A good conversation often stimulates you to remember things you forgot you ever knew.

WAX ON: Read something and imagine you are in conversation with the article. Argue with it! Play devil's advocate. Try Rant, Rave, Report or practice "A to C." Ask yourself if you would like to influence the writer, agree with them, tear them a new one or kindly add to what they have to say?

Journal about and keep track of the how, why, what, when and where of the things you find that work for your journaling practice. Remember that this too will change over time, so be ok with that.

Now it's up to you to learn how to use these tools. I have my ideas, but those are mine, and you've heard enough of that. This is your life.

When all the elements are tools in your tool box, then your creative self is just as accessible as your logical self. Nature isn't always balanced, it makes corrections to *create* balance. Fall, winter, spring or summer all have their ratios of elements. You'll thrive by respecting this.

Time to stop doing and start being.

I hope these tools have helped, and you have moved one step closer to the horizon ...

NOW GO WRITE!

ABOUT THE AUTHOR:

MATT LUCAS is the founder of Yama Systems LLC, TheYamaSystem.com and TotalBSWellness.com. TotalBS stands for Total Balancing Sequence (obviously) as well as the number one rule in skill building: "If you don't show up and practice, it's all BS." He has been a martial artist since age five and a professional musician since age 13. Over the years he has gained students all around the country while touring as a musician and training late nights in parks and college campuses while others ... weren't. After his nomadic fighting bard period, Matt settled in Oakland where he became a member of The Stunt People and opened his dojo *The Open Matt*. Over the past decade as a full-time yoga and martial arts instructor he has been recruited as a trainer and lead stunt performer for the AMC TV Series *Into the Badlands* as well the wellness trainer for *The Matrix: Resurrections*.

Matt's blending of Yoga and Martial Arts, aka "YAMA," is the foundation of his work along with emotional intelligence, empathy training, situational mindfulness, and decision making under stress. Basically it's about building tools for aligning thoughts, words, and actions. His work has been used by fighters, celebrities, law enforcement, children, and adults of all levels. The goal of this work is to heighten our consciousness and expand our capacity and longevity. All of the physical work of martial arts, yoga, and music is balanced out by his love for writing, poetry, journaling, and songwriting.

ABOUT THE DESIGNER: Matt Clark is the co-founder and creative director of a boutique studio focused on storytelling and presentation design (alimat-inc.com) where he helps founders, inventors, CEOs and artists tell their stories and reach their right people. In the past many decades, he's worked in diverse capacities as a creative director, designer, copywriter, editor, photographer and illustrator. Matt is a devoted student of Sifu Matt Lucas (see above, in his natural habitat). In his other life as a fine artist he writes and illustrates children's stories, fills books with found-image collage, and creates strangely psychedelic nature photography with poetic accompaniment under a mysterious nom de plume.

www.ingramcontent.com/pod-product-compliance
Lightning Source LLC
Chambersburg PA
CBHW060757100426
42813CB00004B/859